Study Guide

Catching Fire

The Hunger Games – Book Two

BookCaps™ Study Guide

www.bookcaps.com

Table of Contents

Historical Context

Suzanne Collins was born in Connecticut in 1962. In the 1990's, she wrote from some children's television shows on the Nickelodeon network. While working on a kids' show called "Generation O!" she met writer James Proimos who inspired her to begin writing children's novels. Her first novel, "Gregor the Overlander" was the first in a series of critically acclaimed books known as the Underland Chronicles and was inspired by Alice in Wonderland. The Underland Chronicles were published between 2003 and 2007 and earned Collins notoriety in the literary world. In 2008 "The Hunger Games" was published as the first book in a trilogy that was followed up by "Catching Fire" (2009) and "Mockingjay" (2010); the trilogy has been wildly successful.

Collins' idea for the books of the Hunger Games series came from watching reality television, reading war coverage, and influencing from the times of gladiator battles. The world of Panem, where the novels take place, is a dystopian society in the future where all of the "districts" in which people are dictated by the President who lives in the Capitol; a place far different from the poor districts which exist solely to provide goods for those who live in the Capitol. Every year the Capitol takes two teenagers from each district as tributes to compete in the Hunger Games, a gladiator-type reality show where only one tribute comes back alive. Katniss Everdeen, the heroine of the series, begins a battle against the Capitol that propels itself to a catastrophic degree in an effort to live a life of freedom.

Plot

Several months after the 74th annual Hunger Games have ended Katniss finds herself living in a house much nicer than she is used to with more food than she has ever had in the Victor's Village of District 12. She barely speaks to Peeta and Gale reveals feelings that Katniss never knew he had.

President Snow visits to inform Katniss that she is in a lot of trouble for the stunt she pulled with the berries in the arena, and she must work hard to convince him that she and Peeta are truly in love. During the Victory Tour Peeta and Katniss resume their air of romance and even get engaged for the public.

Katniss finds out that some of the districts have begun rebelling against the Capitol, and she knows that she must fight, not run away as Gale suggests. Katniss hears a rumor that District 13, thought to be destroyed, still exists and wants to go there for a chance to rise against the Capitol's control but Haymitch thinks she is being silly. Katniss finds out that for the Quarter Quell, the 75th anniversary of the Hunger Games, the rules have been changed and only victors will participate in this next Hunger Games, which means definitely Katniss and either Haymitch or Peeta.

It is Peeta who goes and despite the fact that Katniss is determined to save him this time, rather than herself, it seems the other tributes have all decided to save Katniss at all costs; Katniss has become the face of hope in the rebellion that is forming against the Capitol and her mockingjay pin has become a symbol of the rebellion. As the arena crumbles under the rebelling tributes Katniss is rescued, but Peeta is taken hostage by the Capitol.

Characters

Katniss Everdeen

Katniss has just won the 74th Hunger Games along with Peeta, whom she still does not know if she has true feelings for. There is a rebellion stirring after Katniss' actions in the last Games and it has caught the attention of President Snow. When Katniss is thrown into the Games yet again she is determined to save Peeta though everyone else is determined to save her; Katniss has become the face of the rebellion without even realizing it.

Peeta Mellark

Peeta is still desperately in love with Katniss though he is waiting for her to feel the same way. Peeta proposes to Katniss in public to be sure that they still have the support of the nation and stays by her side through the entire Victory Tour and the subsequent Quarter Quell games that they are thrust into, yet again. Peeta works very hard to protect Katniss though, yet again, it is Peeta who needs Katniss to protect him. When the rebellion strikes and the arena explodes Peeta is captured by the Capitol rather than saved by the rebels.

Gale Hawthorne

Gale is on the same page as Katniss as far as a
rebellion goes from day one, as Gale has always had a
problem with the totalitarian government. Gale goes
along with Katniss' suggestion that they run away
with their families, though he gets angry with her
when he finds out that she wants Peeta to come too.
Gale expresses his true feelings for Katniss and
finally kisses her, which only confuses her more.
When Gale is caught hunting by the new
peacekeepers, he is whipped severely in the public
square and Katniss attempts to jump in to save him.

Prim Everdeen

Prim is Katniss' younger sister who has grown so
much in the time that Katniss has been absent because
of her duties with the Games. Prim is developing a
love for medicine and healing, as Mrs. Everdeen has,
and works often with her mother from their kitchen in
Victor's Village which has turned into the doctor's
office of District 12. Prim slowly grows into a
thoughtful and intelligent young woman who serves
as a great source of comfort for Katniss.

President Snow

President Snow is the president of Panem and rules the districts from the Capitol. Snow is furious with Katniss for her performance in the 74th Games because she has challenged the authority of the Capitol and basically proven that she will do whatever she sees fit and cannot be controlled. President Snow threatens to harm Katniss' family if she does not make the world absolutely positive that the berry stunt was an act of love rather than an act of rebellion.

Haymitch Abernathy

Haymitch is the only Hunger Games victor from District 12, other than Peeta and Katniss, who is still alive. He continues to drink heavily after returning to District 12, and urges Peeta and Katniss to keep their love affair public knowledge, even encouraging the engagement which he assures Katniss is necessary as being with Peeta is really her only option in life now. When it comes time for the tributes to be chosen for the Quarter Quell, Haymitch is chosen but Peeta steps up to take his place and Haymitch becomes the mentor once again, who encourages Peeta and Katniss to make allies.

Finnick Odair

Finnick is the tribute, and past victor, from District 4 which is the fishing district.Finnick is very attractive and knows it, and he has quite the charming personality. Finnick's main skills involve swimming, using nets, and throwing a trident. Katniss initially dislikes Finnick because of his arrogance, but he takes her by surprise when he wants to be her ally in the arena. Katniss does not want to trust Finnick, but he seems determined to keep her alive and she does not understand why until she learns about the rebellion.

Cinna

Cinna is the personal stylist who turns Katniss into the "girl on fire". Cinna is unlike other people from the Capitol, as he is very quiet, reserved, and normal in comparison. Katniss becomes great friends with Cinna and has a lot of respect for him as a person and for his creativity. Cinna is a genius when it comes to styling, and when Katniss and Peeta are put into the games a second time it becomes obvious that he has a hint of rebellion in him as well, as he dresses Katniss as a mockingjay for her interview before the Quarter Quell. Cinna is beaten to death right in front of Katniss' face as she is preparing to enter the arena.

Effie Trinket

Effie is the escort for the District 12 tributes, and she comes from the Capitol. Effie is very proper, despite the fact that she has bright pink hair, and gets extremely offended around Haymitch and Katniss with their harsh ways. She at first accepts the Hunger Games as a part of life and a chance to further her career but by the time Katniss and Peeta are to compete for a second time she more emotionally invested in them and tries to become a source of comfort to them as she is sad an angry that they must compete again.

Octavia, Flavius, and Venia

Octavia, Flavius, and Venia are Katniss' prep team from the Capitol. They are the ones who primp, polish, wax, and make-up Katniss before all of her public appearances. Katniss is at first shocked by the startling appearance of her prep team and is disgusted by their trivial, worry-free, and privileged lives, as well as their interest in the Hunger Games. Katniss develops a little respect and even appreciation for her team when she is prepping for her second Games because she sees how emotional they are at the thought of nearly losing her again.

Johanna Mason

Johanna is the female tribute, and former victor, from District 7. Johanna is good friends with Finnick so she allies herself with him as well as Katniss, Peeta, Beetee, and Wiress.Johanna seems to truly dislike Katniss which makes Katniss distrust Johanna more than anyone else. Johanna tells Katniss that she has no one left who she loves, which helps Katniss to understand Johanna's bitterness. At the end, of the Quarter Quell Johanna is captured by the Capitol just like Peeta.

Beetee

Beetee is the male tribute, and former victor, from District 3. Beetee is an older man and Katniss trusts him and wants him as an ally immediately though no one else understands why. Beetee is an accomplished and extremely intelligent inventor who teaches Katniss how to see a force field, something that not many others can do. Beetee has formulated the plan to short out the force field around the arena with electricity and Johanna has nicknamed him "Volts".

Mags

Mags is Finnick's fellow tribute from District 4, and another former victor. Mags is a much older woman who rarely speaks anything that makes sense, though Finnick always seems to understand her and the two of them are very close. Mags was not originally chosen to be in the Quarter Quell, but she volunteered to take the place of Annie Cresta, who is eventually revealed to be Finnick's girlfriend.When Finnick realizes he cannot rescue both Peeta and Mags from the poisonous fog Mags does not hesitate to take her own life by running into the fog.

Mrs. Everdeen

Mrs. Everdeen is the mother of Katniss and Prim who grew up in District 12 though she did not live in the Seam until she was married. When Mr. Everdeen dies in a mine explosion, Mrs. Everdeen becomes deeply depressed though she eventually pulls herself together enough to start her own apothecary from her home in the Seam. Katniss does not have much respect for her mother because of how she fell apart at the death of her husband and left Katniss to fend for her entire family. Mrs. Everdeen becomes the "doctor" in District 12 when the new peacekeepers begin physically punishing people.

Caesar Flickerman

Flickerman is a very famous television reporter in the Capitol. His claim to fame is interviewing the tributes from each district before the Games are to begin. Flickerman is very kind and has a way of making everyone appear likeable and in making everything sound charming. Flickerman's hair color changes each year as the color that represents the Games changes each year. Katniss is at first shocked by his appearance but quickly learns that he is her ally on the stage because he will spin her social awkwardness into something endearing.

Themes

Rebellion

Rebellion is the driving force behind this novel
though Katniss does not realize the magnitude of
what is happening as much of it has been hidden.
During the Victory Tour there are hints that rebellion
is happening and when she meets Twill and Bonnie in
the woods, who are escaping to the mysterious
District 13, she finds out that she and her mockingjay
are the faces of the rebellion that is stirring against the
Capital. The other tributes work hard to save Katniss
in the arena because the rebellion is making a big
move that Katniss and Peeta are not informed of.

Love

Love is a complicated topic for Katniss because she does not know how she feels about either of the boys who are in love with her; Gale and Peeta. Love is something that Katniss has pretended as long as she has been in the public eye, to gain sympathy for herself and Peeta, but while Peeta does not have to fake these feelings Katniss does not know what she is feeling for him, nor for Gale. The only love that Katniss is sure of is that for her sister Prim, and love is what the gamemakers use against Katniss and the other tributes while in the arena; Katniss and Finnick both hear the tortured voices of Prim and Annie in one of the areas of the arena.

Survival

Survival is a constant theme of all three books in the series. The people in the districts are constantly struggling to survive against hunger while the tributes are constantly trying to survive in an arena where they are being hunted. Aside from actual physical survival the rebellion is sparking the idea of surviving emotionally and mentally by rising against the totalitarian government of the Capitol. Katniss never tries to survive herself; she is not interested in running away with Gale and she is not interested in saving herself in the arena, she only wants to save Peeta.

Interdependence

Even more so than in the first book Peeta and Katniss are totally interdependent upon one another. Peeta and Katniss are a team and they constantly work as one, always looking to the other for support and ensuring one another's safety. Katniss becomes a shell of herself when she and Peeta are not speaking after the 74th Hunger Games because she no longer feels complete or seems to know how to function when he is not around, and she is devastated when she learns that he was taken by the Capitol after the Quarter Quell.

Government Control

The government begins to fight back after the stunt that Katniss played in the Hunger Games and asserts their control by announcing that the Quarter Quell will involve only victors of past games; proving that they can make people do whatever they want. President Snow replaces the peacekeepers of the districts with new ones who are very strict and vicious in ensuring that the citizens follow the rules, going so far as to set up a gallows and a whipping post, which Gale must face. President Snow even shows up to confront Katniss face to face on her intentions and threatens the safety of her friends and family.

Loyalty

Loyalty is very important to Katniss because she cares nothing about her own safety and only about the safety of those around her. She hates that she has hurt both Peeta and Gale but refuses to allow her loyalty to either of them waiver. Katniss also wants to remain loyal to the people who see her as a sign of hope, like Rue's family and Twill and Bonnie. While Katniss does not ask for others to be loyal to her, the Capitol basically demands that people be loyal to them, for fear of losing the tight grasp of control they have over the districts.

Sacrifice

Sacrifice is something that is central to all of the books in the series, but especially in this one because so many people are sacrificing themselves. Katniss is always willing to sacrifice herself for others and Peeta is always willing to sacrifice himself for Katniss; but this time everyone is sacrificing their lives for Katniss, as she is the face of the rebellion even though she is not fully aware of it.Basically the entire country of Panem, with the exception of the Capitol and a couple of the lower districts, is sacrificing its livelihood for Katniss and the idea of freedom.

Freedom

Freedom is the reason for the rebellion. The citizens of Panem have been repressed by a totalitarian government for so long and are becoming increasingly uncomfortable with the control that the Capitol has over them. Katniss' rebellion against the Capitol as was televised during the 74th Hunger Games was all that the people of Panem needed to give them a small taste of what freedom would be like. Freedom means no more Hunger Games, no more starvation, and no more barely surviving so other people can thrive.

Anger

Most of the anger comes from Katniss, toward her mother, toward the Capitol, and toward herself. Katniss is angry with her mother for emotionally abandoning her and Prim when their father died though she is trying to sort through that anger. She is also angry with the Capitol for having such control over the citizens of Panem and finding entertainment in something so tragic as the bloodbath that is the Hunger Games. Finally, Katniss is often mad at herself, mostly for the confusion that she feels in her feelings for both Gale and Peeta.

Determination

Determination is one of the most prominent qualities that Katniss possesses though in terms of "Catching Fire" it is the determination of the other victors that is most important. Katniss believes that they will all be determined to win the Games and that she will be their first target once in the arena; what Katniss does not know is that they are determined, but not to win the Games, only to save Katniss because she is the heart and soul of the impeding rebellion, which is about to make a huge move.

Chapter Summaries

Chapter One

Katniss is home and back to her regular routine of hunting and trading, though after winning the Games she no longer has to hunt for food. Katniss slips under the fence into the woods to hunt, the site of a kiss that took place between her and Gale after she returned from the games. Despite the fact that Katniss' family no longer needs food, other families do, like Gale's.

Katniss heads straight to the Hawthorne house to bring them food and then goes to the Hob to trade, buy some healing supplies for her mother, and has a bowl of Greasy Sae's soup. Katniss heads back to the Victor's Village where she, her mother, and Prim now live with Haymitch and Peeta as neighbors. She stops first as Haymitch's house to wake him, knowing he is probably passed out drunk, because this is the first day of the Victory Tour that they must go on.

Peeta shows up as well with bread to coax Haymitch out of bed, and there is obvious tension between Peeta and Katniss. When Katniss gets to her own house, she finds that President Snow is waiting for her.

Chapter Two

Katniss goes into the room where President Snow is waiting for, and the two of them have a private conversation, despite Mrs. Everdeen's reluctance to leave them alone together.

The President tells Katniss that he has heard murmurs that a rebellion may be in the works after the stunt Katniss pulled with the berries at the last Hunger Games. President Snow tells Katniss that she must convince the people of Panem that she acted out of her intense love for Peeta, rather than acting out of defiance for the Capitol. The President hopes that the talk of a rebellion will calm down if people do not think that Katniss is on board.

Katniss is told by President Snow that if she does not do as he says and successfully convince Panem of her love for Peeta then he will kill Gale. Gale has been presented as Katniss' cousin to explain how close they are, though President Snow does not seem to believe it. President Snow hints at the kiss that happened between Katniss and Gale though Katniss does not understand how he could possibly know.

Chapter Three

Katniss sinks into a bath to calm herself before she must begin getting ready for the Victory Tour. As Katniss is bathing, her prep team arrives and immediately fusses over the state of Katniss' nails and body hair since the last time they saw her. As the prep team is working on Katniss, Cinna arrives to dress her.

Katniss is very happy to see Cinna and the clothes that he has designed for her, but which they are going to present as Katniss' designs because she needs to have a talent to present on the Victory Tour. As Katniss is dressing, Mrs. Everdeen enters with the mockingjay pin that Katniss wore through the Games; a gift from Madge. As the tour begins Katniss and Peeta revert back to their very convincing, loving relationship that will surely convince Panem of Katniss' motives; a though that is in the back of Katniss' mind since President Snow's visit. The first time the train stops for gas Katniss pulls Haymitch aside and tells him about the visit she got from the President.

Haymitch tells Katniss that she has to go along with it, and a life with Peeta is really her only option at this point; she must let go of her feelings for Gale.

Chapter Four

As Katniss prepares to be presented to the public her prep team waxes every bit of hair from her body, and it gives Katniss time to think about her future, and the possibility of any children she has being subjected to the Hunger Games. Katniss is uncomfortable with the idea of the first stop on the tour, which will be District 11 – Rue's district.

At breakfast, Peeta and Katniss decide to be friends again and Peeta shows Katniss his paintings, as painting is the talent he will be presenting. Katniss finds that Peeta has painted the games, which terrifies her despite the fact that she is in awe of his talent. Once they arrive in District 11 they are immediately ushered into trucks and brought to the Justice Building.

They are expected to make a speech in front of the District 11, but Katniss does not know what to say to the families of Rue and Thresh. Peeta takes over and tells the families that each of them, per year, will get one month of his and Katniss' yearly earnings, which shocks everyone and makes Katniss proud. Katniss thanks the District for Rue and Thresh and also for the bread they sent. A man in the crowd whistles Rue's mockingjay tune and the entire district gives Katniss the three-finger salute of District 12.

After Katniss leaves, she has to run back to grab her flowers and she sees the man who whistled Rue's tune being shot in the head by a peacekeeper.

Chapter Five

Peeta and Katniss are brought back into the Justice Building rather quickly, and they learn that the newsfeed ended after Katniss spoke, so no one else in Panem heard the song, saw the salute, or saw the man get shot.

Haymitch takes Katniss and Peeta on a hasty tour through the justice building until they end up in the dome, where Katniss realizes there must be no cameras or microphones; he tells Katniss to share with Peeta what the President told her. Peeta is mad that Katniss did not tell him before and makes a new rule that there will be no more secrets between then, which Haymitch thinks is a good idea.

The trio goes to the ceremonial dinner in District 11 that evening and head to the train that night to be off to their next location. Over the next couple of weeks, Peeta and Katniss visit with all of the other districts and put on a great show of their love for one another.

At night, Peeta starts sleeping in Katniss' bed to comfort her as she has been having nightmares since the Games. Once they arrive in the Capitol Peeta proposes to Katniss in front of all of Panem, but when Katniss makes eye contact with President Snow he slightly shakes his head to let her know that she is not convincing him.

Chapter Six

While in the Capitol Peeta and Katniss are put through interviews and learn that President Snow has, for some reason, decided he would like to throw their wedding. Katniss and Peeta act the perfect couple at the celebration dinner that night though Katniss is horrified and disgusted at the amount of food that is being thrown away, knowing how many starving people there are in the districts.

During the celebration Plutarch Heavensbee, the new head gamemaker, asks Katniss to dance and she does so, though she does not want to. He shows Katniss his pocket watch which has a mockingjay on the face when he runs his finger over it, which does not seem odd to Katniss because she has seen a lot of jewelry emblazoned with mockingjays, though she does feel a certain intensity coming from Heavensbee that she does not understand.

Katniss and Peeta are ushered back onto the train after the celebration dinner and are brought back to District 12 for the Harvest Festival. As Peeta and Katniss are getting ready in the Mayor's house, Katniss sees the television monitor in the Mayor's office flicker on; on the television Katniss sees the alert of an uprising that has happened in District 8, which she definitely was not supposed to see. Katniss quickly leaves the office and pretends she is looking for Madge while the Mayor excuses himself because he sees his television screen flash on, undoubtedly showing him exactly what Katniss just saw.

Chapter Seven

The next day Katniss leaves a message for Gale to
come to the cabin by the lake where her father used to
take her. When Gale comes he does not want to speak
to Katniss at first, as he is upset by her engagement,
but he listens when Katniss tells him of her visit from
President Snow and his threat on Gale's life.

Katniss tells Gale that she wants to run away with
him and their families, which Gale quickly agrees to
and he tells Katniss that he loves her. Katniss does
not return Gale's sentiment and also tells him that she
wants Haymitch and Peeta to come with them as well,
because she could not possibly leave them behind.
Gale gets mad at Katniss when he hears that Peeta
will be coming and tells her that she can do more
good in the world by rebelling rather than running.

Gale runs off and when Katniss gets back to town she
finds Peeta walking to his parent's house, and tells
him of her plans to run away, which he agrees to.
When they get to town, they find that Gale is being
whipped in the square by the new head peacekeeper.

Chapter Eight

Katniss runs to the square and jumps in between Gale, who is barely conscious, and the whip which hits her in the face. Haymitch tells the peacekeeper that he has to leave Katniss alone because she is a victor and it will not look good for him to beat one of the victors. One of the other peacekeepers, Darius, arrives and tells the new head peacekeeper that Gale has received more than enough punishment for his crime and should be let go.

Peeta, Haymitch, and a couple of the miners, who Gale works with carry him to Katniss' house so Mrs. Everdeen can treat his wounds. Katniss finds out from Haymitch that Gale was being punished because he was caught poaching a turkey, which is something he has always done and has always been ignored by the previous head peacekeeper because Gale's hunting benefitted the entire community.

Katniss expects the peacekeepers to come and arrest either her or Gale all night, but no one shows up other than Madge, who brings medicine for Gale which makes Katniss a little jealous, as she thinks that perhaps something is going on between Madge and Gale. A relentless snowstorm comes that buries District 12 and as Katniss sits by Gale's side watching him heal she decides to stay and fight rather than run away. She kisses Gale as he is in medicinal haze and hopes he does not realize it.

Chapter Nine

Katniss weighs her options and thinks of all the things that the Capitol could take from her if she were to fight back, but she realizes that they have already taken so much from her. Katniss is left alone with her thoughts for days while she waits out the storm, and when she finally leaves the house she meets with Peeta and Haymitch to discuss and uprising.

Haymitch thinks that Katniss is crazy, and an uprising would never work because there are not enough people in District 12 to fight against the peacekeepers who would be sent stop the rebellion. When they get into the town, they realize that whipping posts and stockades have been set up in the square. They see smoke in the distance and realize the Hob has been burned down. After a visit to Gale's mother, they find that no one uses her laundry services anymore, her youngest child has measles, and no one will speak to Katniss anymore because they fear punishment.

Katniss decides she needs some time alone at her father's cabin, but when she approaches it she finds a woman in a peacekeeper's uniform, holding a piece of bread with a mockingjay on it.

Chapter Ten

The woman at the cabin is not alone, she is
accompanied by another woman, and they are not
peacekeepers but refugees from District 8. The two
women worked in the factory which made
peacekeeper uniforms and had been planning to
escape for a while, slowly stealing pieces of the
uniforms for one of the women and her husband so
they could disguise themselves when they finally did
escape.

The woman's husband was killed, and the factory was
bombed; the women managed to escape the district
with their uniforms, and everyone assumed they had
died in the explosion. The women are heading to
District 13 to join forces with those who survived the
destruction there, though to Katniss' knowledge there
are no survivors in 13 so she does not think they are
going to find anything there.

Katniss teaches the women some survival skills, as they are obviously starving, and she also leaves them with some of her food and wishes them luck. As Katniss heads back to town, she finds that the fence has electric current running through it again and she does not know how she will get back.

Chapter Eleven

Katniss decides that the only way around the fence is to go over it. She walks along until she finds a tree that looks all enough and sturdy enough to help her cross over. Katniss gets across the fence and as she drops to the ground she feels intense pain, knowing that she has badly injured the heel of her foot as well as her tailbone.

Katniss knows that she must pretend she is not injured or she will blow her cover, as she is not supposed to be in the woods. As an alibi, Katniss stops at the shops and picks up some stuff for her mother and Prim before heading home. Katniss finds two peacekeepers at her house waiting for her return and launches into a story about getting lost while trying to find a goat keeper who has a goat to impregnate Prim's goat Lady with, blaming Prim for giving her bad directions.

After the peacekeepers accept her story and leave her alone Katniss reveals her injuries, which Mrs. Everdeen treats before Katniss heads to bed. While Katniss heals over the next few weeks she and Peeta add to the book of edible plants that Katniss' father began; Katniss describes the plants and Peeta draws pictures of them. Katniss watches a news report from District 13 one day and realizes that the footage they use is old, as the same mockingjay flies by the corner of the screen in every report, as though the Capitol creates fake reports over old footage to convince the rest of Panem that there is no one in 13.

Chapter Twelve

Katniss is to have a photo spread done modeling six wedding dresses which the President has chosen for her. The people of Panem and the President will decide which dress Katniss should wear in her wedding to Peeta. The prep team gets Katniss ready for her shoot, which frustrates her because it takes so long.

The day after the shoot Katniss tries to speak to Haymitch about the possible existence of people in District 13 though Haymitch does not seem to think it is possible. That night everyone has to watch a mandatory program on the television, which is of Katniss' photo shoot, and it is followed by an announcement from the President giving the rules of the Quarter Quell, the 75th annual Hunger Games.

Every 25 years there are special rules for the Quarter Quells to remind the people of the Dark Days before the Games. Supposedly the rules for all Quarter Quells were made at the start of the games and have been locked away. At the 25th anniversary, the districts voted for tributes, at the 50th anniversary there were double the number of tributes and this year, the 75th anniversary, the tributes will be chosen from each district's living victors; Katniss will be going into the Games again and will be accompanied by either Peeta or Haymitch.

Chapter Thirteen

Katniss runs from her house, horrified, and hides in the basement of one of the abandoned houses in Victor's Village. Eventually Katniss comes out and goes to see Haymitch, who thinks that she is there to ask him to go in and save Peeta but all Katniss does is ask him for a drink.

Katniss gets drunk and stumbles home where she sees Gale and wishes that she had run away with him when she had the chance. Gale puts Katniss to bed, and she sleeps late the following day. Despite the fact that Katniss has an awful hangover, she heads to Haymitch's house and finds that Peeta is already there and he is throwing away all of Haymitch's alcohol.

Peeta tells Haymitch and Katniss that neither of them are to drink anymore, and they all have to start training for the Games right away. The three train together over the next few weeks and Gale even helps by teaching them to make snares. On the day of the reaping, Haymitch is drawn as the male tribute, but Peeta comes forward and volunteers to replace Haymitch. All three of them are ushered onto a train with Effie, and none of them wanted to say goodbye to their families before they left.

Chapter Fourteen

Once on the train Peeta, Katniss, and Haymitch are in game-mode and sit to watch the reapings from the other districts; Katniss is especially intrigued by an old lady named Mags from District 4 who steps into to take the place of a younger girl. They watch the tapes of their competitors from each one's Hunger Games victory to study their strengths and weaknesses.

Katniss has trouble sleeping because she is suffering nightmares again and heads back down to the lounge where she finds Peeta still watching the videos. They decide to watch the video of Haymitch's win in the Games, curious as to how he was victorious. Haymitch was allied with his co-tribute from District 12, a girl who was a good friend of Mrs. Everdeen. Haymitch found a way to use the force field around the arena to his advantage, which is how he won; Katniss realizes that Haymitch has shown his rebellion against the Capitol before, and his defiance could greatly aid Katniss in saving Peeta.

Peeta and Katniss realize that Haymitch has caught them watching the video, but he is not angry at them, though seemingly angry at the Games.

Chapter Fifteen

As the prep team gets Katniss ready to present herself
in the Capitol they cry incessantly at the idea of
possibly losing her again. Katniss complains to Cinna
about the tears, and he promises that he will speak to
them about it. Each year the tribute must dress for the
opening ceremony to represent the industry for which
their district is known; for District 12 it is coal
mining.

Cinna sticks with his theme from the previous year of
dressing Katniss to represent not a coal miner, but
coal itself and she is put into a suit that appears to be
a glowing, burning, piece of coal. As Katniss is
waiting by her chariot Finnick Odair, the tribute from
District 4 who is ridiculously good looking,
approaches her and makes a pass, though he leaves
when Peeta comes over. Katniss and Peeta hold hands
throughout the ride, but they do not smile and wave
as they did the previous year.

In the elevator back at the training center Johanna Mason, the tribute from District 7, strips naked and rides up with them. Finnick finds it hilarious that Katniss is so innocent that people cannot help but to try to tease her. Katniss is only angry until the elevator door opens and she finds herself facing her favorite peacekeeper from District 12, Darius, who has been turned into an Avox.

Chapter Sixteen

Katniss is very upset to find that Darius has become an Avox and her sleep that night is interrupted by nightmares, once again. In the morning, Katniss is feeling quite rebellious but Haymitch convinces her that she must come to training and it would be beneficial for her and Peeta to ally herself with other tributes before the Games begin, though Katniss has no desire to do so.

At the rope station, Katniss is approached by Finnick who teaches her a particularly complicated knot; Finnick knows a lot about knots because he is from the fishing district. At the fire building station, Katniss meets Beetee and Wiress, the older tributes from District 2 whom she takes an instant liking to despite the fact that she knows Haymitch will not approve of them as allies. Beetee teaches Katniss how to see a force field, which not many people can do.

Katniss has to sit with everyone at lunch, and to her dismay she begins to like the other tributes which she will, unfortunately, be involved in a bloodbath with soon. On the final day of training, Katniss does not know what to do for the judges so she hangs a dummy from the ceiling and writes "Seneca Crane" on it in blood-red paint. Seneca Crane was the previous head gamemaker who had been killed, which was covered up, after he allowed both Katniss and Peeta to win the previous Hunger Games.

Chapter Seventeen

When Haymitch finds out about Katniss' stunt in the judging room he is not happy; nor is he happy when he learns that in judging Peeta drew a picture in dyes of Rue's body after Katniss had covered it with sunflowers. Both Peeta and Katniss get top scores from the judges which Haymitch knows is just the judges' way of painting a target on both of them in the eyes of the other tributes.

The next day Katniss and Peeta are allowed to relax, and they spend the day having a picnic on the roof. The following day it is time for interviews with Caesar Flickerman and President Snow requests that Katniss wear the wedding dress he chose for her. Katniss remarks that the dress is quite heavier than she remembers, and Cinna informs her that he had to make some alterations. When Katniss finally takes the stage to give her interview, she takes the cue from Cinna to twirl and show off her dress; as she does so the entire thing seems to go up in flames, and when they clear what remains is a gown inspired by a mockingjay.

Chapter Eighteen

Katniss knows that Cinna has placed himself in a world of trouble by making this statement and she silently appreciates him but worries about him all the same. The crowd is beside themselves with sadness over the fact that Katniss and Peeta will never be able to get married as one of them will soon die but Peeta surprises the audience by telling them that he and Katniss are already married in their minds.

Peeta says that they performed a traditional marriage ceremony in District 12, though it is not legally binding; then he shares with the audience that Katniss is pregnant with his child, which catches Katniss by surprise. At the end of the interviews the tributes all take stage together, and, as a symbol of unity, they all join hands before the audience. The Capitol is outraged as this show of solidarity and sends everyone home who is not directly involved in the games.

The next morning Cinna dresses Katniss for her second turn in the Games and puts her into the tube that will bring her to the arena. The tube closes, but Katniss is not sent up to the arena right away, instead she is stuck watching as Cinna is beaten and dragged away by peacekeepers. Katniss is send up into the tube, in total shock, and finds herself in the middle of a huge body of water; the message to Katniss seems clear, a "girl on fire" cannot survive in water.

Chapter Nineteen

Katniss realizes that each tribute is standing on a platform in the water and must swim to a land arm that connects to the cornucopia; Katniss feels fortunate that she knows how to swim because she is sure that many tributes do not. When Katniss arrives at the cornucopia she finds that Finnick is the only other one there, but he seems to be wearing a gold bracelet just like the one she saw Haymitch wearing so she thinks he is supposed to be her ally, though she does not trust him.

Finnick saves Katniss from the District 5 man, and she takes the opportunity to take a bow and arrows from the stockpile of supplies. Katniss works with Finnick to fend off some of the other tributes. They soon realize that the cornucopia has nothing but weapons, no survival supplies, so they take as many weapons as they can.

Katniss sees Peeta still standing on his platform because he does not know how to swim so Finnick goes to rescue him and then gets Mags and the four of them quickly retreat. Katniss climbs a tree to check out the situation and sees that several tributes have died at the cornucopia. They decide to look for fresh water, but as they are walking Peeta walks straight into a force field and falls to the ground.

Chapter Twenty

Peeta's heart has stopped beating so Finnick performs some sort of strange act of breathing into Peeta's lungs (CPR, though Katniss has does not know what it is called) to bring him back to life as Katniss screams and begs for him to come back to her.

After Finnick saves Peeta they decide they must find water now, especially because Peeta is weakened. Finnick asks Katniss how she knew a force field was there because he saw that she was about to yell before Peeta ran into it, and she tells them that she can hear the electricity with the ear that the Capitol fixed for her after the last Games; this is not true though, Katniss learned how to see force fields from Beetee.

They walk the perimeter of the force field, and find no water so they take the slope downward and decide to make camp for the night.Katniss goes out on her own and sees an animal in a tree that looks like a rat, and his mouth is wet; Katniss knows there must be water somewhere. Finnick and Mags have created a shelter for the four of them, and Katniss gives Peeta the rat creature she killed to cook for dinner.

That night eight faces are shown in the sky and Katniss realizes there are only eight of them left in the arena. Katniss gets a gift from a sponsor, and it is recognized as a spile; Katniss realizes she has to tap the trees for water and it works. As Katniss keeps watch that night, she hears a loud gong sound go off twelve times and struggles with what it could mean. Soon a fog comes over their camp that makes Katniss' skin blister.

Chapter Twenty-One

As Katniss, Peeta, Finnick, and Mags all run from the fog they realize that not only is it blistering their skin but it is also taking control of their nerves, making it difficult to have control over their bodies.Peeta and Mags are affected the worst, and cannot walk for themselves so Finnick carries Peeta and Katniss tries to carry Mags. Katniss cannot hold Mags for very long and Finnick knows he cannot carry both, which he tells Mags; to Katniss' shock Mags gives Finnick a kiss on the cheek and runs into the fog, killing herself. As the three stumble to the water's edge to escape, the fog Katniss realizes that the salt water greatly soothes her blisters and she shares this information with Peeta.

The two of them have to drag Finnick into the water because he is hurt worse than they are and cannot move for himself. Peeta goes to tap a tree and Katniss realizes that the monkeys in the trees seem to be congregating together, and staring down at them. Katniss calls to Peeta but as soon as he moves the monkeys attack. Katniss uses all her arrows and asks Peeta to throw her more, and he drops his knife in the process. Unarmed, Peeta is nearly attacked by a monkey but the girl from District 6 jumps in between Peeta and the monkey, saving him and badly injuring herself.

Chapter Twenty-Two

As the monkeys retreat, Katniss, Peeta, and Finnick try to help the girl who saved Peeta, but her wounds are too severe and they just keep her company and hold her hand while she dies. Katniss offers to keep watch so Finnick can rest that night, but he refuses, insisting that she sleep and Katniss can tell that Finnick wants some time to be alone so he can grieve for the loss of Mags.

In the morning, Katniss' blisters itch terribly so she asks for Haymitch to send her something and only moments later she receives some tar ointment that looks atrocious but soothes the itching. Finnick catches some shellfish for breakfast, and the trio sees three other people stumbling out of the woods coughing; Katniss recognizes them as Johanna Mason from District 7 and Beetee and Wiress. Johanna seems to dislike Katniss and tells her that she only saved Beetee and Wiress for her, which Katniss does not understand. Beetee has injuries that Katniss attends to and Wiress keeps babbling incoherently "tick, tock, tick, tock".

That night Katniss sees the lightning accompanied by twelve gongs sounds again and realizes what Wiress is trying to tell them; the arena is a clock.

Chapter Twenty-Three

Katniss tells everyone what Wiress has discovered; each section of the arena corresponds to a time on the clock and in each section of the clock a different kind of attack happens – the fog, the monkeys, etc. They decide to sit at the cornucopia and watch the different sections of the arena to see what each section does and at what time.

At the cornucopia, they restock their weapons and Peeta draws a picture of the arena in the sand so they can keep track of the sections. As they are distracted, the tributes from Districts 1 and 2 attack; Katniss and Johanna manage to kill the tributes from 1 but not before they kill Wiress.

The tributes from District two hide behind the cornucopia and Katniss chases after them but the island they are all standing on begins to spin out of control and everyone is forced to hold on for their lives. When the island stops spinning, Finnick saves Beetee from the water and Katniss swims out to Wiress' body to get the wire that Beetee found in the cornucopia and seems so important to him.

The five who are remaining head back toward the jungle and despite Katniss' uneasy feelings she goes off with Finnick to get water while Peeta stays on the beach with Johanna to make another clock drawing. In the jungle, Katniss hears Prim's screams.

Chapter Twenty-Four

Katniss runs after the voice and soon realizes that
Prim's scream is coming from a jabberjay, a
genetically mutated bird, and Katniss kills the bird.
When Finnick comes after her, he too hears the voice
of someone he loves and runs off in the other
direction. As Katniss and Finnick run away they
come to a wall that does not let them get away from
the birds, they have to wait until that section of the
clock is done with its torture. Katniss and Finnick are
both convinced that their loved ones are being
tortured by the Capitol, and their screams were
recorded, but Beetee assures them that it would be all
too easy for the government to create the false
screams of anyone they want.

That night they watch the faces of the dead flash in the sky and receive a gift of rolls from District 3. Beetee is sure to count the rolls before anyone eats them, and they decide to save some of them for later. Peeta and Katniss keep watch together that night and Katniss finds that Peeta has brought a locket with him that contains pictures of Mrs. Everdeen, Prim, and Gale; he uses the locket to try to convince Katniss to let him die to save her but Katniss refuses.

Chapter Twenty-Five

The next day Katniss tries to convince Peeta that they have to break away from the others because they will have to kill them soon enough, but Peeta thinks that they should wait. Beetee comes up with a plan that day to kill the District 2 tributes; he will run his wire from the lightning source that strikes at midnight into the water and kill the tributes when they are on the beach.

They all hike up to the lightning tree together, and Katniss tells them where the force field is so they stay away; Beetee is amused when the others tell him that Katniss can hear the force field because he knows that he taught her how to see it. After Beetee is done examining the tree, and the area around it they all go back to the beach where they dine on seafood and more rolls that have been sent from District 3.

Chapter Twenty-Six

The next day they all head to the lightning tree so Beetee can rig the electrical wire. Beetee tells Johanna and Katniss to run down to the jungle, carefully placing the wire, so they can quickly head off to section one of the clock where they will be safe. Katniss does not want to leave Peeta behind because she still worries that the others are going to turn on them and separating them will create the perfect opportunity; however, Katniss and Johanna are the fastest so it makes the most sense.

Halfway down the hill Johanna gives the wire to Katniss and shortly after the wire snaps back at Katniss and she finds herself being thrown to the ground with a hard blow; Katniss is barely conscious, but she can feel that Johanna is sitting on her and digging her knife into Katniss' arm. When Katniss comes to, she is sure that her fears have been realized and she runs back up the mountain to get Peeta.

Katniss finds Beetee unconscious with wire securing a knife to his hand, and she remembers what Haymitch told her before she left for the Games – to remember who the real enemy is, which Katniss knows is the Capitol. Katniss wraps the wire around one of her arrows and shoots it into the force field; sure that is what Beetee was trying to do.

Chapter Twenty-Seven

Lightning strikes and Katniss sees the arena start to fall apart right in front of her eyes. A hovercraft comes and takes Katniss out of the arena, and she finds herself in the presence of the head gamemaker before she passes out. When Katniss comes to she finds herself in a medical room and Beetee is in the bed next to her; she is sure they have been captured by the Capitol. Katniss feels that Peeta must be getting tortured, so she grabs a syringe that she plans to use to kill him so he will not suffer, and goes down the hall.

Katniss hears Finnick's and Haymitch's voices coming from another room along with the head gamemaker, Plutarch Heavensbee. Katniss reveals her presence and she is told that there was a plan in place all along to rescue Katniss from the arena and many of the other tributes had made their promise to save Katniss and Peeta at all costs, even if it meant their own lives. Katniss has become the face of the rebellion, and she needs to live to spark hope in others and they knew that if Peeta did not survive then Katniss would not be a strong enough leader.

Katniss finds out that Peeta was not rescued by them; however, because the Capitol got to him before they could, and also finds out that they are on their way to District 13 where people are still living and the rebellion is stationed. Katniss is devastated by her fear for what is happening to Peeta in the Capitol and confused at the new information. Gale comes into the room, injured, and tells Katniss that her family is fine but District 12 has been destroyed.

About BookCaps

We all need refreshers every now and then. Whether you are a student trying to cram for that big final, or someone just trying to understand a book more, BookCaps can help. We are a small, but growing company, and are adding titles every month.

Visit www.bookcaps.com to see more of our books, or contact us with any questions.

94667508R00046

Made in the USA
Columbia, SC
28 April 2018